Disaster Dan

Michael Wagner

Illustrated by
Adam Nickel

One warm summer morning in Sunshine Heads, the Murphy family was surprised to feel the earth beneath their house suddenly shake.

All three of the Murphys—six-year-old Kaylan, twelve-year-old Suzie and their mum—immediately stopped what they were doing and looked at each other.

When the windows finally stopped rattling, Kaylan asked his mum, "What was that?"

"I'm not sure, darling," said Mum. "I think it was an **earthquake**, but we don't normally get them here."

Suzie was about explain that she'd recently learned in school that earthquakes can happen anywhere, but the rumbling began again before she could speak. This time it was louder. It even moved the kitchen table.

"It *is* an earthquake!" said Suzie. "We're meant to get under the table. That's the safest place."

Under the table, Kaylan started singing a little song to calm his nerves:

"Got a crisis on your hands? Disaster Dan!
Nature ru-in-ing your plans? Disaster Dan!
If a quake is on its way,
He will come and save the day.
Disaster Dan, Disaster Dan, Disaster Dan."

"What are you singing?" asked Mum.

"It's an ad for Disaster Dan," explained Suzie. "You call him if there's a disaster."

Mum reached up and grabbed her phone from the kitchen table. She left a message for Disaster Dan to come and help. The moment she ended the call, the rumbling stopped.

The Murphys had barely climbed out from under the table when Kaylan noticed a red van pulling into the driveway.

The family rushed outside to find that Disaster Dan had arrived.

"What seems to be the problem, Murphy family?" he said, as he lowered his sunglasses.

"There's an earthquake!" said Kaylan, excitedly.

"I'll be the judge of that," said Disaster Dan, squatting down to inspect the driveway. "It would explain these cracks in the concrete."

"Yeah," said Kaylan, dropping onto his belly to study the driveway. "An earthquake explains it."

"Cracks are classic signs of a quake," said Disaster Dan. "These little nasties happen because earthquakes make the ground wobble like jelly. Cracks can open up anywhere. Usually they're tiny hairline cracks like these, but sometimes they're big enough to swallow a whole car."

Kaylan crawled away from the cracks.

"Actually," said Suzie, "I think those cracks are because of the drought. There's been hardly any rain for years so the ground has dried up, and that's made it shrink. Anything sitting on top of the dried ground, like our driveway, probably has cracks in it now. So, yeah, they're because of the drought."

Disaster Dan took his sunglasses off so he could get a better look at Suzie.

"Well that's a nice little story," said Disaster Dan. "Who told you droughts can crack up the ground?"

"My science teacher, Mrs Vesuvius," replied Suzie. "Droughts can even cause dust storms, and bushfires and all sorts of bad things."

Disaster Dan shook his head and smiled.

"Well, let's hope your Mrs Vesuvius is right, young lady. Let's hope the cracks in this driveway were caused by a little old drought and not some *big, scary earthquake*!"

Suzie cringed and quietly said, "Um, yeah, let's hope so."

BEEP! BEEP! BEEP!

"Oh," said Ms Murphy. "That's the oven timer. My chocolate mud cake must be ready."

"Can you come in and tell us more about earthquakes?" Kaylan asked Disaster Dan.

"That's what I'm here for, son."

"Yes!" said Kaylan, dragging Disaster Dan through the front door.

Kaylan dragged Disaster Dan all the way to the kitchen, where Mum was placing her freshly baked mud cake on the table.

"No touching it until it's cooled," she said.

"Want to stay for morning tea?" Kaylan asked Disaster Dan. "Mum's mud cake is the best."

Before Disaster Dan could reply, the house began to rumble.

"Quick everyone!" yelled Disaster Dan. "Under the table!"

The Murphys and Disaster Dan squeezed under the kitchen table. Disaster Dan quickly rolled up his sleeve and looked at his watch.

"Ten … eleven … twelve," he counted.

The rumbling stopped.

"I make that fifteen seconds," Disaster Dan said. "And my guess is a **magnitude** of, oooh, two point three. Maybe two point four."

"A magni-tube of what?" asked Kaylan.

"Magnitude," said Disaster Dan. "It describes how big something is. That's how we measure earthquakes."

Kaylan frowned at Disaster Dan. "How can you measure a rumble?"

"It's called the **Moment Magnitude scale**," Suzie explained. "Mrs Vesuvius told us about it in class. The scale tells you how powerful an earthquake is. It goes from one to ten. In the old days they used the **Richter scale**. The most powerful earthquake ever measured was nine point five. That's really big! People could feel that earthquake from thousands of kilometres away. The earthquake we just felt was much smaller."

"Aren't you clever, Suzie?" said Ms Murphy.

"Thanks, Mum," said Suzie.

"The quake we just experienced was *nothing* compared to a nine point fiver," said Disaster Dan, as if he were correcting Suzie, rather than agreeing with her. "And you seem to have forgotten the **Mercalli scale**. Did Mrs Vesuvius tell you about that one?"

"I was just getting to that," said Suzie. "The Mercalli scale measures the impact of a quake on people ..."

"Oh, really?" interrupted Disaster Dan. "It measures the impact on people does it? I think you'll find the Mercalli scale measures the impact on all sort of things: Earth's surface, nature, buildings *and* people—the whole kit and caboodle."

"I was about to say that," said Suzie.

"Of course you were," said Disaster Dan with a knowing grin.

"The rumbling stopped a while ago, Disaster Dan," said Mum. "Can we hop out now?"

Disaster Dan poked his head out from under the table. He sniffed the air as if he could smell an earthquake. Then he pulled his head back in and said, "Settle in, folks. This could take some time. Call it a sixth sense or just an instinct for disaster, but something tells me we haven't seen the last of that quake yet."

"Good," said Kaylan. "I like talking about earthquakes."

"Good man," said Disaster Dan. "Always make the best of your situation, no matter how dangerous or life-threatening it really is."

Kaylan gulped. Mum put her arm around him. Suzie rolled her eyes.

"Now, let's make the best of this situation," continued Disaster Dan. "It's not every day that ordinary folks like you get to sit down with an expert like me. Is there anything you'd like to know about disasters?"

Kaylan put his hand up.

"Fire away," said Disaster Dan.

"What's an earthquake anyway?" asked Kaylan.

"Well!" Disaster Dan said, looking surprised. "Let me explain."

Disaster Dan reached up and quickly grabbed the mud cake from the kitchen table. Sliding it onto his hand, he then placed it abruptly on the floor in the middle of everyone and asked, "Now what do you see here?"

"My chocolate mud cake," said Mum.

"Our morning tea," said Suzie.

"*Yuuuuum*," said Kaylan, licking his lips.

"Open your eyes, people!" ordered Disaster Dan. "That's not a cake! It's the Earth's **mantle**!"

"Can I have a piece of mantle?" Kaylan asked.

"You wouldn't want to eat mantle, son," replied Disaster Dan. "Mantle is made of boiling hot, oozing, squelching rock and metal. It's so hot down there that rocks and metal are turned to liquid! It's a swirling, disgusting mess!"

"Hey!" said Mum.

"Stay with me here, folks," said Disaster Dan.

He held the cake up to his eye level and peered at it intensely.

INNER CORE 1300 KM THICK
OUTER CORE 3000 KM THICK
MANTLE 2300 KM THICK
CRUST 5-70 KM THICK

"And where do you think this oozing, boiling pit of horror is? Well, it's right under our feet."

Kaylan lifted his feet off the floor.

"It's okay, Kaylan," said Suzie. "It's at least five kilometres below the ground. You can't feel it at all."

Kaylan looked at Disaster Dan. He nodded, so Kaylan gingerly put his feet back on the dining room floor.

"In some places, Earth's mantle is seventy kilometres below the surface," Suzie explained to Kaylan. "And it's very, very thick, like three thousand kilometres or something. Then, if you keep going past the mantle, you get to the two **cores**—the inner core and the outer core. So it goes, **crust**, mantle, outer core, inner core. And the crust is what the land and sea sit on. Mrs Vesuvius taught us all that."

"Well, did Mrs Vesuvius teach you this?" said Disaster Dan, reaching up to grab a plate from the kitchen table. "Look away now, people!"

As everyone turned their faces away, Disaster Dan smashed the plate on the floor, breaking it into four pieces.

"Now what do you see?" he asked.

"My good crockery!" complained Mum.

"Ms Murphy," said Disaster Dan, "is this the right time to be worried about crockery?"

"Um," said Mum. "I guess not."

"Thank you," said Disaster Dan. "Now, what do you see?"

Disaster Dan arranged the pieces of broken plate on the mud cake.

"Our morning tea being ruined," said Suzie.

"I'm not hungry any more," grumbled Kaylan.

"Oh, I get it," said Mum. "That's Earth's crust, sitting on the mantle."

"A gold star for you, Ms Murphy," said Disaster Dan. "In fact, it's what we experts call the **tectonic plates**."

"What sort of plates?" asked Kaylan.

"Tectonic," replied Suzie. "They're part of Earth's crust. They sit just below the land and ocean."

"And," said Disaster Dan, taking over, "there are seven very large tectonic plates plus many more smaller ones wrapped all the way around the planet, fitting together like a jigsaw puzzle."

"I love jigsaw puzzles," said Kaylan.

"I hope you love tectonic plates, too," said Disaster Dan. "Because those plates are the only thing keeping us safe from all that boiling, oozing mantle."

"I love tectonic plates," said Kaylan. "They're amazing."

"Well, don't love them too much, my young friend," said Disaster Dan. "Because they are a very long way from being perfect."

"Okay," said Kaylan. "I only love them a bit now."

"Wise man," said Disaster Dan. "Because those tectonic plates are broken. Just like your mum's plate. They're *smashed*! Which is why we have earthquakes."

Kaylan looked at Disaster Dan. "Huh?"

"I know this is hard for ordinary people to understand," said Disaster Dan, "so allow me to demonstrate."

Disaster Dan lightly pressed on two pieces of the broken plate. As their edges rubbed against each other, they squeaked slightly.

SQUEAK. SQUEAK.

"Hear that?" he said. "Listen closely."

SQUEAK. SQUEAK.

"I think Mum's cake is crying," said Suzie.

"That's an earthquake!" said Disaster Dan. "Only quieter. When the edges of these two plates rub together, they squeak and vibrate under my fingertips. It's exactly the same with tectonic plates. Every now and then, when they rub against each other, we hear a squeak and a vibration too. Only the squeaking is much louder and the vibration can make your house fall down."

"I hate tectonic plates now!" said Kaylan.

"I know where you're coming from," said Disaster Dan. "But it's really only the edges you should hate. They're the dangerous parts. Luckily, here in Australia, we're not close to any of those rotten edges."

"Phew," said Kaylan.

"BUT," said Disaster Dan, "we are only a couple of thousand kilometres from the most dangerous edge of all, the one they call the RING … OF … FIRE!"

"*Eek!*" said Kaylan, shuffling closer to his mum.

"What's the **Ring of Fire**?" asked Kaylan. "Will it get us?"

While Disaster Dan chuckled, Suzie answered her little brother's question.

"The Ring of Fire," she said, "is the edge of a big tectonic plate that pretty much has the Pacific Ocean sitting on it.

Most of the world's earthquakes, **tsunamis** and **volcanoes** happen along its edge. It is like a big arc that goes past countries like Japan, Chile, the USA, Canada, Indonesia and New Zealand."

"Yay!" said Kaylan. "You didn't say Australia! That must be why we hardly get any earthquakes!"

"Hold on there, young man," said Disaster Dan. "We get our fair share of earthquakes, don't you worry about that!"

"Australia has a major earthquake about every five years," continued Disaster Dan."And little ones about every fifteen months."

"But mostly where hardly anyone lives," added Suzie.

"Lots of people live in Sunshine Heads" said Kaylan. "Are we having an —?"

Before Kaylan could finish his sentence, the house started to rumble again.

"Brace yourselves, people!" ordered Disaster Dan. "This could be the big one!"

The rumbling stopped almost instantly.

"What magnitude was that one?" Kaylan asked .

"I'm not a human **seismograph**," laughed Disaster Dan.

"A human what-ma-what?" asked Kaylan.

"Seismograph," said Disaster Dan.

"It's what they use for measuring the power of earthquakes," added Suzie."And other little rumblings."

"The technical name for those rumblings is **tremors**, Suzie," said Disaster Dan."And that last quake was probably about one point one on the scale. Not too bone-rattling, just a little reminder of the extreme power of nature."

"I don't like nature any more," said Kaylan."It's too extreme for me. I wish earthquakes only happened in the ocean. Then no one would ever have to hide under tables."

Disaster Dan looked at Kaylan for a moment, and then said,"If only you knew how wrong you are."

Kaylan's face crumpled.

"I didn't mean to hurt your feelings," said Disaster Dan, "but earthquakes at sea are among the most dangerous of all. They can trigger a tsunami."

Kaylan frowned at Disaster Dan.

"Before you ask, Kaylan," said Suzie. "A tsunami is a giant wave—a really, really, really big one."

"How can an earthquake make a wave?" asked Kaylan.

"It happens out at sea," said Disaster Dan "The tectonic plates move because of all that oozing mantle. It pushes them around a bit. When they move, they rub up against each other, Earth rumbles, it stirs up the ocean, and if it's a big enough rumble, it stirs up a tsunami!"

"When that happens," continued Disaster Dan, "you have to get away from the shoreline and get up as high as you can. You have to run to the hills, or climb the nearest staircase. Just get high up! And then wait until the wave passes. That's all you can do to save yourself from a tsunami."

Kaylan snuggled closer to his mum.

"And that's not all! Whatever you do," continued Disaster Dan, "*never* go down to the shoreline after the first tsunami. There is almost always a second one coming, and sometimes more. Do *not* go back to the shoreline. Have you all got that?"

Mum, Suzie and Kaylan nodded.

"I don't think I've emphasised the incredible danger of tsunamis enough," said Disaster Dan.

"Oh, I think you have," said Ms Murphy, clinging tightly to both of her children.

"No," said Disaster Dan, "There are few more things you need to know. Back in 2011, a huge earthquake off the coast of Japan triggered an enormous tsunami."

"I remember that," said Ms Murphy, sadly. "It was horrible."

"What happened?" asked Kaylan.

"The world changed forever," said Disaster Dan. "I'm not exaggerating. Not only did the tsunami kill thousands of people and set the Japanese economy back billions of dollars, but the earthquake actually moved the whole island of Honshu a couple of metres further out to sea. Can you believe that? The earthquake was so big, it moved an island."

"Wow!" said Suzie and Kaylan.

"And it broke off a whole section of Honshu's coastline," continued Disaster Dan. "Snapped it right off!"

"How awful," said Mum.

"And under the ocean," said Disaster Dan, "right at the centre of the quake, the seabed is now completely different. It's changed forever. Forever!"

"*Whoa*," said Kaylan.

"But the most amazing thing of all," said Disaster Dan, "is that the Japanese quake moved the whole planet. Scientists have calculated that the earthquake was so powerful it altered the distribution of Earth's mass. That made the Earth rotate a tiny bit faster, which makes our days a fraction shorter. Isn't that crazy! One earthquake changed the length of every day!"

"Is that true?" asked Suzie in amazement. "Mrs Vesuvius never said that."

"It is," said Disaster Dan. "Time only changed by a fraction of a second, but it did change. An earthquake of magnitude nine, close to the surface, is a powerful thing. And so is a tsunami the size of an office building. That's what happened in Japan in 2011."

Disaster Dan bowed his head. The others looked down too. They had a moment of respectful silence.

"Do we have tsunamis in Australia?" asked Kaylan, when his nerves had calmed down.

"We only have a low risk of tsunamis," replied Disaster Dan.

"Phew," said Kaylan, looking slightly more relaxed.

"But we have records of at least forty," said Disaster Dan.

Kaylan tensed again.

"But not one death," said Disaster Dan.

Kaylan's shoulders relaxed again.

"We don't have much to fear from tsunamis in Australia, Kaylan," said Disaster Dan, gently.

"Yes!" said Kaylan.

"But those things, on the other hand," said Disaster Dan, pointing out the window to the nearby mountain range. "They can do some serious damage right here!"

"Mountains?" said Mum. "What can they do?"

"Those peaceful mountains," said Disaster Dan, "hide a nasty little secret. You see, they're actually volcanoes. All three of them. Three big time bombs, ticking away."

The Murphy family gasped.

"Oh, they've been **dormant** for thousands of years," said Disaster Dan. "But a volcano is a volcano, and no one knows when these three could suddenly go *Boom!* and blow their tops sky high!

"Imagine it—a river of boiling hot **lava** spewing out from Earth's mantle and right down this street."

"Can I have my teddy, Mum?" asked Kaylan.

"And that river of molten lava could flow this way as it heads for the ocean," continued Disaster Dan. "Wouldn't that change the landscape? The street covered in basalt rock.

Brand-new rock formations all over the beach. The mountains could even lose their pointy peaks. What a sight!"

"Can we stop talking about volcanoes now please, Disaster Dan?" asked Mum. "You're scaring Kaylan."

"Oh, don't worry about volcanoes, young man," said Disaster Dan. "No Australian volcano has erupted for thousands of years. Well, not on the mainland."

Kaylan let go of his mum, saying, "It's okay, Mum."

"Then again," said Disaster Dan, "scientists think there may be a link between earthquakes and volcanic eruptions. So, you never know—today's earthquake could just fire up those dormant volcanoes."

"Oh, no!" said Kaylan. "There's going to be hot lava!"

BRIIING! BRIIIING! Disaster Dan's phone rang.

"Disaster Dan, your man for a crisis, speaking," he said.

"Hi Dan," said a man's voice through the speaker. "I'm still digging the foundations, but did you want that extra one in the western corner?"

"Of course I do, Chris," said Disaster Dan. "I want Disaster Dan's Crisis Theme Park to have strong foundations. You dig all the holes you can!"

"Okay, boss," said Chris. "In fact, I'm digging one right now."

Suddenly the earth rumbled again. Everyone braced themselves. The windows rattled. The broken pieces of plate slid off Mum's mud cake.

Then it quickly stopped.

"That's probably deep enough," said Chris, over the phone. "Oh, maybe a bit more."

The ground rumbled again, but only for a couple of seconds.

"Done," said Chris. 'That's deep enough."

A look of horror slowly came over Disaster Dan's face. He turned away from the others and whispered, "Just dig one more hole for me, Chris."

"Anything you say, boss. Digging now."

The earth rumbled.

"Stop!" ordered Disaster Dan. The earth stopped rumbling.

"Sure, boss," said Chris. "So how are things going? What's the crisis?"

"Got to go," squeaked Disaster Dan, ending the call.

Disaster Dan slid out from under the table, saying, "Safe at last!"

The Murphys crawled out too.

"It wasn't an earthquake at all, was it?" said Mum, standing up.

"It's just all the digging going on next door!" said Suzie.

Kaylan popped up, looking confused.

"No charge for today's consultation!" announced Disaster Dan, as he headed for the front door.

"I should think not!" said Mum, following him.

Disaster Dan raced out of the house, adding, "Another crisis averted thanks to Disaster Dan!"

He climbed into his van and pulled out of the driveway.

"What about my broken plate!?" called Mum.

"And our mud cake?" yelled Suzie.

"I'll give you a free family pass once Disaster Dan's Crisis Theme Park is built!" shouted Disaster Dan through his side window. Then with a wave and a squeal of tyres, he headed for the building site next door.

"Well, that's just great!" said Mum.

"I can't believe it, Mum," said Suzie.

"Me neither," said Kaylan. "We actually met Disaster Dan, and he's the coolest man in the world!"

Glossary

core the centre of the Earth

crust the outer layer of the Earth

dormant a volcano that has not erupted for thousands of years but could erupt again

earthquake when the surface of the Earth shakes and vibrates because of underground movement

lava liquid rock that comes out of a volcano when it erupts

magnitude size

mantle the region of the Earth between the crust and core

Mercalli scale a scale that measures the damage made by an earthquake

Moment Magnitude scale a scale for measuring how powerful an earthquake is

Ring of Fire a zone of frequent earthquakes and volcanic eruptions around the edge of the Pacific Ocean

seismograph an instrument that detects and measures the size of an earthquake

tectonic plates large pieces of rock that form the crust of the Earth, like a jigsaw puzzle

tremor a slight earthquake

tsunami a large ocean wave caused by an earthquake under the ocean

volcano an opening in the Earth's crust through which hot gases and molten rock shoot out during an eruption